THE
Archive Photographs
SERIES

LONG EATON

Central Wesleyan Football Club, 1929-30.

Compiled by
John Barker

BATH • AUGUSTA • RENNES

First published 1994

The Chalford Press
12 Riverside Court
Bath BA2 3DZ

ISBN 0 7524 0010 6

Typesetting and origination by
The Chalford Press
Printed in Great Britain by
Redwood Books, Trowbridge

Contents

Acknowledgements

A special thank you to the people who have provided me with their photographs and spent the time to come and share their memories of 'Old Long Eaton', to the Library Service of the Derbyshire County Council and the staff at the Long Eaton Library, and to the Curator and Friends of the Erewash Museum.

Thanks to Mr G. Chmielinski, Mr I. Jacklin, Mr J. Rudd, Mr A. Heath, Mr J.B. Hickling, Mrs G. Holmes, Mrs P. Hutchins and Mrs M. Talbot, and also to Mr Mick Goy for all his help and patience in assembling this collection of photographs.

Introduction

The official opening of the new *Long Eaton Advertiser* offices on West Gate happened to coincide with the paper's jubilee celebrations. Through the opportunity of researching old copies of the paper, I felt that the following recollections painted a very accurate picture of 'old Long Eaton.'

From the Jubilee Supplement of *The Long Eaton Advertiser*, 1883-1933:
'During fifty years the sweeping changes in Local Government have given birth to numerous public authorities, and, instead of the Old School Boards, we have Education Committees, Public Assistance Committees following on after the demise of the Poor Law Guardians. The growth of motor traffic in recent years has given us an entirely new authority in the Traffic Commissioners. The old Sanitary Authorities, the Local Boards, Highway Boards and Boards of Health have been replaced by the Urban and District Councils, but the Parish Council is still with us'.

From the J.B. Maskell Recollections, in the Jubilee Supplement:
'From 1865, when I commenced my duties at Messers S.J. Claye's Works, where I continued for 48 years, in that year the works were being considerably extended, and were finding employment for a large number of men.

'Starting from the railway crossing we should first notice the iron gates leading to Manor House, in which Mr and Mrs Claye and their family then resided. Across the brook were two farmhouses, Bramley's and Edward White's, on the site of which now stands Claye's Erecting Shops. The Home Closes of these two farms are now built on: Acton Road, Nathaniel Road, Oaklee Mills. The cattle pound and pinfold was hereabouts. On the right hand side of Main Street were 6 villas built by Mr Claye, and tenanted by Mr Newsum, Mr Gaskin and other officials. On the opposite side the only buildings were Mr Maltby's house, Heap's grocers shop, and the Old Barn Chapel, with some old cottages. The Primitive Methodists commenced their services in Chapel Street, and in the same street were the first gas works, which had an unfortunate start, the gas-holder being blown over in a violent gale. This part later became the Co-operative stables. Other old cottages led up to the Bush and Maltby Lace Factories. On the East side there was one house and 4 small cottages between Mr Newsum's and Station Street Corner. The two corners of Station Street were allotment gardens, and a small farmhouse, Tebbuts, stood where Zion Hall and Chapel were built. A row of almshouses called the 'Little Row' occupied the site where the Post Office and some big shops have since been erected. On the West side a footpath, called the 'Twitchell' led from Station Street towards Sawley Lane, passed some old cottages called Temperance Row. This site is now filled by the Royal Hotel, West Gate, and the new Advertiser buildings.

'The first National School was built in 1864, on land given by Mr Claye. On the North end of the Market Place, where the National Provincial Bank stands, was the house for the former Parish Clerk, Mr Hickinbottom. Opposite, what is now Regent Street Corner, was an old farmhouse belonging to Mr John Smith, who was Churchwarden for over 50 years. This site is now occupied by the Westminster Bank.

'Over the Canal Bridge (in what is now Derby Road) there were no houses in 1865, only fields and gardens. A solitary farm stood somewhere near where Canal Street is to-day. The Vicarage was the first house built on Wilsthorpe Lane (Derby Road) and others gradually followed.

'Across the railway (Toton Gates) the old 'Coffee Pot Hall' was the only house in the Nottingham Road District.

'The three canal bridges at that time were of the steep, narrow, switchback pattern, similar to those at Draycott and Sandiacre. Owing to traffic increase they have been replaced by wide, modern structures at Derby Road, Tamworth Road and Longmoor.

'The cemetery was opened on Saturday 2 April 1884. The land for this, and also West Park, was purchased from the Harrington Family.

'The 'eighties were the days of the old Long Eaton Rangers, who defeated all comers, and included winning the Birmingham Cup among their virtues, beating West Bromwich Albion in the Final.

'Cricket was also a popular game in those days.

'The river Trent is sometimes a dangerous neighbour, and many serious floods have been experienced. One of the worst was in 1875, when the writer had the experience of helping to navigate some of the side streets on a raft and handing coal, bread, etc, to the imprisoned householders through the bedroom windows.

'The National School was the only school till 1876 when the High Street Board School was opened.

'Long Eaton had much to thank the Midland Railway Company for amidst the worst depressions of the staple trades, the railway men must have helped to keep things going, and Toton Sidings has been a remarkable mainstay to the District. In 1865, The Midland Line commenced at Hitchin and the passengers for the Midland Counties departed from King's Cross. Third class passengers on the slow train took 5 to 6 hours to go from London to the Erewash District. Trent Station was opened 1862, and trains from the South usually divided into 3 sections, one to Nottingham, one to Derby and the other for Chesterfield and the North.

'The lace trade has seen many ups and downs, and in its most prosperous periods the machines would be going 20 hours a day.

'There are numerous small businesses of great variety in the town.

'One is the tobacco business introduced by Mr Josiah Brown when he came to Long Eaton in 1871, a genial and popular character, an excellent musician and a fine bass singer.

'Rowland Hill, who came into public notice a few years later, was also gifted with great vocal and musical abilities

'Speaking of music, when I retired from the position of organist at the Parish Church in 1907, after 38 years service, I thought that I had established a good record; but that record has since been exceeded. Mr E Swift has played at Zion Church for nearly 50 years, and Mr Carver at Station Street Baptists 52 years. There are others in the musical world who are so well-known that it is hardly necessary to refer to them, but the names of Mountney, Garnett, Pattison, Turner and Gaze-Cooper may be sufficient to indicate the high musical standard that Long Eaton has reached in these latter years.

'Old established families in the town have done their part in making Long Eaton what it is today, including the Wallis family, Smith's, Crowes, Sheldons, Parkers, Winfields, Hooleys, and others too numerous to mention.

'Those of us who are spared to look back from 1934 to 1865 can realise the remarkable changes that have taken place during that period. If any of the present generation were able to come back and look round in about 70 years time what sort of a place will long Eaton be then say, in the year 2004 AD.'

John Barker
November 1994

One

Recollections — in the Beginning

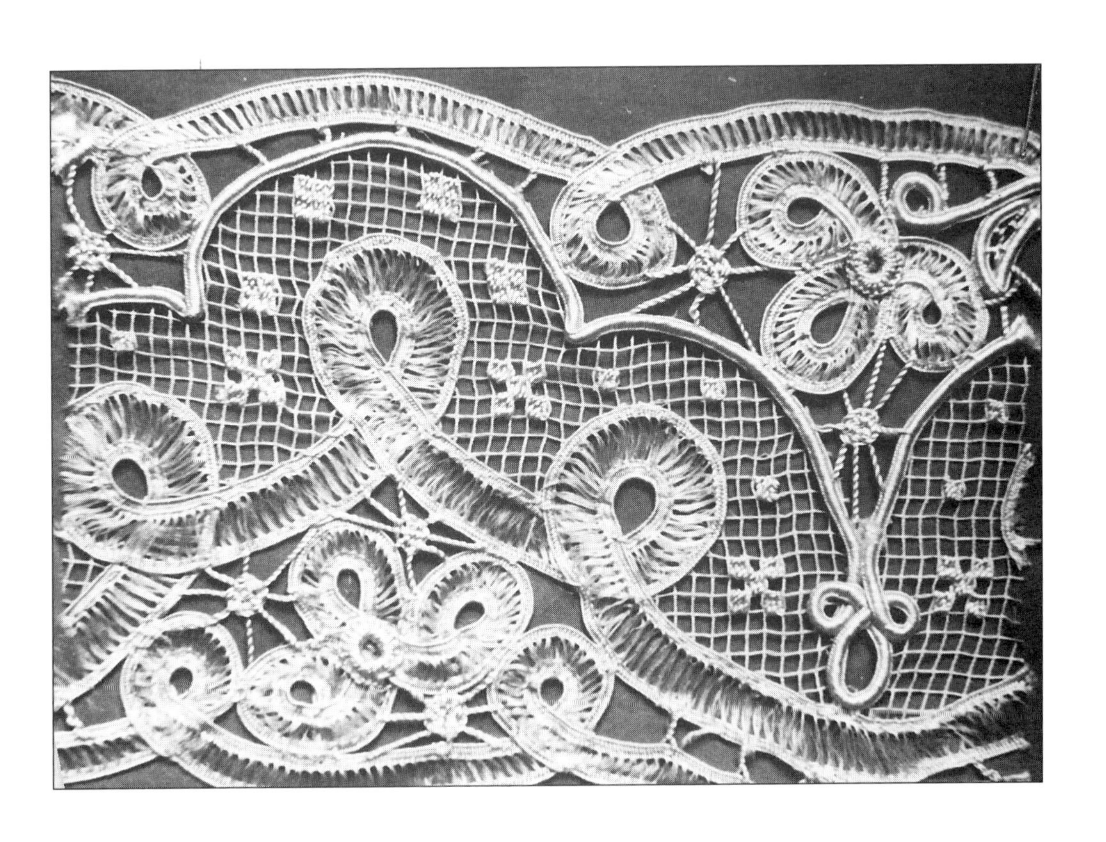

Where waters meet. The lush meadows of the River Trent, looking across to the village of Old Sawley, with the Erewash Canal joining the river at Trent Lock, the Cranfleet Cut in the right

foreground and the Trent about to join the River Soar, below Red Hill. Little has changed here since the Roman invasion.

Old Sawley Village. On the left (below) The White Lyon Inn, with the Nag's Head in the background, two of the few remaining landmarks on the old Nottingham to Tamworth road.

The Erewash Navigation Inn. Built in 1791 at 'Waters-meet': Erewash Canal, the Soar, the Trent, the Derwent and three counties, Derbyshire, Nottinghamshire and Leicestershire.

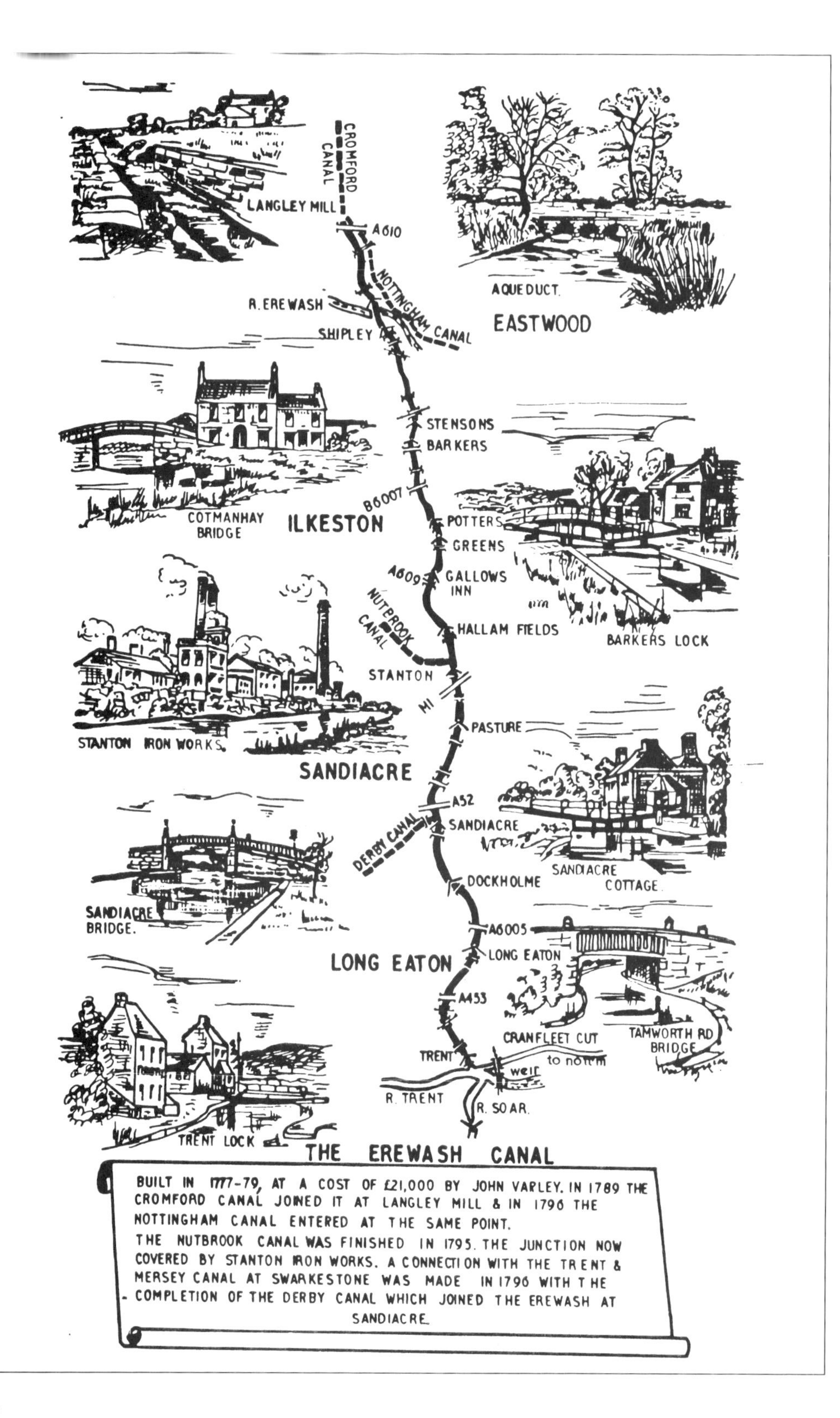
CROMFORD CANAL
LANGLEY MILL
A610
NOTTINGHAM CANAL
R. EREWASH
SHIPLEY
AQUEDUCT
EASTWOOD
STENSONS
BARKERS
B6007
COTMANHAY BRIDGE
ILKESTON
POTTERS
GREENS
A609
GALLOWS INN
NUTBROOK CANAL
HALLAM FIELDS
BARKERS LOCK
STANTON
M1
PASTURE
STANTON IRON WORKS
SANDIACRE
A52
SANDIACRE
DERBY CANAL
SANDIACRE COTTAGE
SANDIACRE BRIDGE
DOCKHOLME
A6005
LONG EATON
LONG EATON
A453
CRANFLEET CUT
TAMWORTH RD BRIDGE
TRENT
weir
R. TRENT
R. SOAR
TRENT LOCK
THE EREWASH CANAL
BUILT IN 1777-79, AT A COST OF £21,000 BY JOHN VARLEY. IN 1789 THE CROMFORD CANAL JOINED IT AT LANGLEY MILL & IN 1796 THE NOTTINGHAM CANAL ENTERED AT THE SAME POINT.
THE NUTBROOK CANAL WAS FINISHED IN 1795. THE JUNCTION NOW COVERED BY STANTON IRON WORKS. A CONNECTION WITH THE TRENT & MERSEY CANAL AT SWARKESTONE WAS MADE IN 1796 WITH THE COMPLETION OF THE DERBY CANAL WHICH JOINED THE EREWASH AT SANDIACRE.

The Bridge Inn and Barker's Lock. The Barker family photographed outside the old Bridge Inn on the Awsworth Road. Since 1779 the crews of narrow boats navigating the Erewash Canal have found rest and refreshment in the bar of this old inn, standing on the banks of this ancient waterway. For almost two centuries working boats stood at the hostelry's moorings loaded with coal, iron and other goods from the thriving industrial region spanning the Derbyshire-Nottinghamshire border. One of its duties as a waterborne coaching inn during the golden age of canal transport was to provide stabling for the horses which plodded the towpaths pulling narrow boats laden with up to thirty tons of cargo. An inn may have been on the site for about a century before the canal was completed in 1779. The lock is said to be named after an owner who sold the canal company the adjoining land now crossed by the canal, stretching nearly twelve miles from Langley Mill to Trent Lock, and built during the great industrial boom which gathered momentum in the second half of the eighteenth century.

TRENT STATION.

The new form of transport. Businessmen were quick to see the potential of the new form of transport, by rail, originally for moving goods and then passengers, the numbers increasing throughout Queen Victoria's reign. Great efforts were made to provide for the needs of first-class passengers. The facilities offered to poorer customers left much to be desired. They travelled, very often in carriages open to the elements, without seats, and often only allowed on the slowest trains, which stopped at every tiny station and dawdled in the sidings. The Midland Railway provided new, luxurious First Class coaches in 1847, and at the same time they abolished Second Class and upgraded travelling conditions for the Third Class, with newly-built carriages with comfortably upholstered seats. Luncheon baskets could be obtained from some railway hotels for passengers in the days of non-buffet cars. However there were refreshment stops at main stations, as at Trent, where a hold of half an hour allowed the passengers the choice of either First or Third Class dining rooms. The original station for Long Eaton was near Meadow Lane crossing. This was so far out of the way that, for the convenience of the upper part of the village, another, called Toton Station, was opened where the Nottingham Road bridge now stands. Both were superseded by one on Station Street. It was the making of the Erewash Valley Branch that roused the village from its long rural repose and started it on its career of expansion and activity. A few years after the opening of the railway, Toton coal siding was made. This initial movement was accelerated by the establishment of Messrs S.J. Claye and Co.'s Wagon Works. 'Claye's Works' have done much for the making of Long Eaton.

The first lace workers. Mr Wootton and Mr Bush, uncle and nephew, emigrated in 1836 to Long Eaton from Gotham, bringing the first lace frame to be housed in a cottage. It could be worked by hand, and it was not until 1842 that the Industrial Revolution made its first impact on the village in the shape of the first factory with a steam engine for power. Mr Bush also introduced coal gas. The first lace factory and those of a later date were small, but Mr Joseph Austin, building his factory in 1852, had a large, four storey building, on land near the market place and the Durham Ox public house. By 1911 at least thirty-nine lace mills and factories had been built in the town.

The Church of St. Laurence, which occupies a central site off the Market Place, can boast a history going back at least nine centuries. For most of its life it was a comparatively small chapel of ease, dependent, like a number of other churches in the area — Breaston, Wilne, Draycott, Hopwell, and Risley — on the great mother church at Sawley. By 1864, with the coming of the railways and the growth of the lace industry, Long Eaton was transformed from a sleepy rural hamlet to a bustling industrial town, and the community had acquired sufficient identity and status to be made into an independent ecclesiastical parish. The time was ripe to enlarge the church, ready to accommodate new and larger congregations.

Mount Tabor in the Market Place. The new Mount Tabor chapel was officially opened in October 1884, replacing the old building of fifty years earlier, which was out of all harmony with modern requirements, being uncomfortable, badly ventilated, and much too small.

The Wesleyan Methodists' first preaching room is said to have been in the old manor house owned by Lady Trowell, who, if not herself a Methodist, must have been in favour of the cause, and as it grew new quarters had to be found, usually in some large kitchen. The opening of their first chapel was in 1852 on Cross Street; it was known as Brown's Chapel, facing Brown's Road. In September 1884 the Wesleyans at Long Eaton had for some time been using their old chapel premises for Sunday School purposes, and as the building became more and more inadequate a fund-raising movement was set up.

Signatures from the past. A bedspread of red and white cotton squares with, embroidered on the edge, the details that it was worked by Mrs Enoch Wallis for the Bazaar in aid of Derby Road Mission Room, Long Eaton, Xmas 1890. Each of the 238 squares bears the signatures embroidered of those making donations, amounting to £34 13s 6d, average 2s 11d per square. The amount raised by exhibiting the bedspread at the bazaar was 12s 6d, and by sale to Mrs Emmiline Wallis of The Spinney, Long Eaton, £3 5s 0d.

The Long Eaton Primitive Methodist Sunday School Band of Hope, photographed beside Bourne Chapel. The Movement was associated originally with the Nottingham First Circuit, a room over a joiner's shop in Long Eaton being used. The membership grew and in 1854 a small chapel was erected in Gas Street, later to be known as Chapel Street. This building soon became too small, and was enlarged. Once again the congregation increased and in 1873 the present building was erected. The site was the gift of Mr Samuel Claye, who also gave a cheque for £100, the pulpit and the Gothic tracery window in the front. The building cost £1,800 and there was seating for 500 people.

The Boys Brigade. Members outside Bourne Church, Stanley Street, *c.* 1907.

Richard Booth snr made a model of the church in shells. He belonged to one of the founder families of the chapel.

Grandma Booth.

Leonard, Arnold, Arthur, Fred, James, Dennis, and Edgar Booth.

Olive Booth, sister to the 'Seven Brothers' Booth.

The new National School was built in 1862 on a site presented by Mr S. Claye of the wagon works. The new school, costing £864 and for 260 children, was enlarged in 1889 to accommodate 287 boys and 238 infants. The school was closed in 1964 and demolished in 1966, to be replaced by St Laurence Infant and Junior School, Collingwood Road, 1972.

The growth of Long Eaton. The following extract is taken from the exercise book of Clarrie Bates, aged 12 in 1919, a pupil at Wellington Street school. 'The word "Eaton" is derived from the word "Aitone", it means an island, "Tone" means an enclosure or a town, thus "Eaton" means a town on an island. About thirty to forty years ago (about 1880) Long Eaton was a very pretty, country village, with its thatched cottages and village pump. It has been a place that has made rapid strides as regards industries, and sanitary conditions; as it is one of the most up-to-date places as regards cleanliness. There have been many fine structures erected such as, the Library, Schools, Churches, places of amusement and one storey factories which are most beneficial for the health of the workers. There are many other fine buildings. Many years ago up the College way it was all green fields and open country, but now there are some of the finest residential villas'. On the front row, fourth from left, is Mrs Grace Heath (née Winfield). 1912.

The foundation stone of Trent College was laid in 1866 by the Duke of Devonshire, in an elevated position, close to the tiny hamlet of Wilsthorpe. As the industrial growth of the town increased, so the demand for housing, with Long Eaton's West End residents stretching to and engulfing the farms in the hamlet. The educational work commenced in 1868. The Revd T. Ford Penn was the first headmaster. Dr Gower, a very talented musician and organist, was on the College staff for several years, and was also captain of the local Volunteer Corps, formed in 1870. The school chapel was erected in 1875 and a splendid view is enjoyed from the terrace on the south front, overlooking the playing fields, and the vast expanse of the town's West Park.

Trent College caught fire in the early hours of 22 July 1922. Fortunately, although three dormitories, a dining hall and a large area of the roof were destroyed, there was no injury to the occupants. The fire brigade spent several days ensuring that no further outbreaks took place. A new fire alarm had been installed earlier that year comprising nine alarm boxes, operated by breaking a glass and pulling a handle, thus registering a signal in the fire station. A telephone inside each box allowed the caller to give more details to the brigade.

The first Council or School Board was opened in High Street in 1867. This school had accommodation for 179 boys and 179 girls and 212 infants, but this was soon insufficient and after only six years additional rooms were in use at Bourne Street Church Sunday School. It is said that the High Street School was built as a psychological antidote to the National School so that children of non-conformist families could find an 'intellectual home with harmony of doctrinal code'. The teaching of handicrafts was particularly stressed under the first headmaster, J.W. Chambers of Radford. In 1929 the school became mixed, boys and girls no longer being taught separately.

Two

Scrap Book and Family Album

Picture postcards. The plain 'post card' was introduced in 1869. Earlier, in the 'fifties, the forerunner of two familiar types of postcard, the photographic view and the portrait photograph, the 'carte-de-visite', were produced which people exchanged with friends. These were followed by portraits of celebrities, but most people associated picture postcards with views of seaside resorts and as mementoes of the grand tour of European countries. By the end of the century members of the Royal Family, politicians, stage celebrities, and the young actresses who appeared in musical comedies, the Edwardian Gaiety Girls, appeared on postcards and these became best sellers in Britain.

The scrap book and family album. As these became more and more popular, so the number of photographers producing material for it grew and families overseas kept in touch with photographs. Photography boomed, and studios were established in almost every street in every town in the British Isles. The carte-de-visite was at first a formal photograph designed only to present the likeness of the subject, but soon the studio setting became fashionable as photographers vied with each other for trade. The Victorians were great collectors and portraits were intended for family albums. Queen Victoria set the pattern and even the humblest of her subjects attempted to follow her.

W.W. Winter, an artist in photography, patronised by Her Majesty the Queen: 'Mr Winter has pleasure in intimating to the inhabitants of Long Eaton and surrounding district that his studio is now replete with all the latest improvements for the production of first-class portraiture, and to those desirous of a pleasing and faithful likeness he would respectfully solicit a sitting'. Midland Street, Derby. January 1884. As photography became more popular and cheaper the outdoor wedding group became the fashion, taken in beautiful gardens or outside the bride's home. Collecting picture postcards was the first of the indoor collecting hobbies to enjoy popularity.

Fashions for children. Influenced by the angelic group on a picture postcard from the turn of the century, the infants were dressed in 'high fashion' (families unknown).

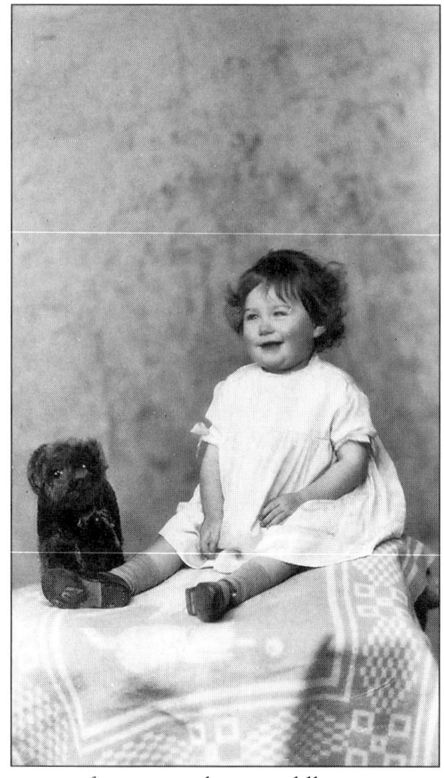

A quarter of a century later, toddlers were allowed a greater freedom of movement. Top left: Young master Barker, on a visit to Derby, models the latest in knitted rompers for an entry into the Family Album. Top right: A few years later a very happy little girl, June, enjoys all the attention of the photographers. Bottom left: A birthday card, 'wishing good fortune on your birth day, and thereafter'.

Royal wedding. Princess Mary, daughter of King George V and Queen Mary, was married in Westminster Abbey on 28 February 1922 to Lord Lascelles. The dress was of silver lamé, veiled with marquisette, embroidered with English roses in a lattice pattern with pearls and brilliants. It is thought that the original embroidery may have been the work of local 'outdoor workers'. Sawley has always been known for the beautiful 'flossed silk' embroidered wedding veils.

Overleaf, pages 40 and 41: In the early days in Sawley, a small number of women possessed lace frames and used to sit outside their homes in summer, working designs on plain net, from paper patterns underneath. Working in the style of a 'lace runner', they used a satin stitch which lies on top of the surface, giving a relief effect. A meeting was arranged with the Curator of the Museum of Childhood, an extension of the Victoria and Albert Museum, located in Bethnal Green. A department houses a splendid collection of wedding dresses and the Princess Royal's wedding dress was displayed in a glass case in order that a photograph might be taken to study the original embroidery. Certainly this is in flossed silk, then heavily re-embroidered with seed pearls and crystals. It is thought that the Court Dressmaker would instruct a local lace maker to use outdoor workers to employ the same method of handling the fabric as the old lace runners had done for years.

Celebrations for the coronation of King Edward VII and Queen Alexandra. The town concludes the coronation celebrations with the roasting of an ox (below). By pressing the trousers down the front and back of the leg instead of down the side, the new King introduced a sartorial innovation. He was also responsible for the introduction of the Homburg hat to Britain, the hat being named after the German spa often visited by the King. Queen Alexandra was also a leader of fashion: by tipping her straw boater forward on her head she soon had all the girls in England copying her style. In June 1912, Queen Alexandra introduced 'Rose Day'. Young ladies dressed in white collected money on the streets of London by selling rose emblems in support of charity.

Anyone for tennis? Edith Heathcote with family and members of the Roper family.

Sergeant Harry Churchill Beet VC, sitting outside the Regent Inn with comrades after the Boer War. Harry is wearing the bush hat.

LONG EATON'S

"Welcome Home"

Banquet,

PEOPLE'S HALL, TUESDAY, Oct 14, 1902.

Name Harry Churchill Beet

Address 135 Sawley Road
Long Eaton

Rank Sergeant V. C No. 3530

Regiment 1st Batt. Sherwood Foresters

YOU are cordially invited to attend this Banquet, given in your honour, in order that your Fellow Townsmen may meet you to express their hearty appreciation of the services you rendered your Country in connection with the late South African War.

The soldiers return from war, and Long Eaton's 'welcome home banquet' was held at The Peoples Hall, on Tuesday 14 October 1902: 'You are cordially invited to attend this banquet in your honour, in order that your fellow townsmen may meet you to express their hearty appreci..tion of the services you rendered your country in connection with the late South African War.'

The *Long Eaton Advertiser*, 5 September 1902: 'The Victoria Cross: how it is bestowed'; accordir.g to the Army List of 1 January 1902, on that date 131 officers and 75 of the lower ranks were entitled to wear the Victoria Cross.

King Edward died in May 1910 and Prince George, Duke of Cornwall and York was proclaimed King George V, with his wife, the former Princess Mary of Teck, as his consort. In December 1911 there was the Great Delhi Durbar, when the King and Queen received the homage from princes and rulers of Indian states. An entirely new crown had to be manufactured as the Crown of the Kingdom, the Imperial Crown, is not allowed to be removed from the kingdom. After the Durbar the new crown was brought back to England and housed with the other regalia in the Tower of London. Lord Curzon of Kedleston was Viceroy of India at this time.

The War Years, 1914-18. On 28 June 1914, the heir to the throne of Austro-Hungary, the Archduke Franz Ferdinand, was assassinated at Sarajevo. Very soon only Italy and England remained aloof from the general European war. England strove to confine war to the Balkans, but was brought into the struggle on 4 August 1914 after the German violation of Belgian neutrality. Italy joined in on the side of the Allies in 1915.

The First World War brought a type of postcard particularly popular with soldiers on the Western Front, who sent them home to their wives and sweethearts. Silk embroidered cards, with sentimental messages and embellished with sprays of flowers and foliage, have been lovingly treasured over the years.

The Great War changed everything: way of life, attitudes, society, politics. People changed too, both mentally and physically. No war had ever involved so many civilians and fashion in clothes and much else was turned upside down and no longer flowed in natural progressions and reactions. The First World War emancipated fashion, but while it was happening the breeches of farmerettes and land girls, the trousers and overalls of the women munition workers and bus conductors, the uniforms of the nurses, post women and the police force, were not considered a part of fashion. Thus fashion dawdled in its tracks while simultaneously it hopped a decade and didn't catch up with itself until the mid-'twenties.

Vintage Transport. The Long Eaton Women's Voluntary Aid Detachment (below) presented a second ambulance to the town to commemorate the Red Cross Hospital they had organised between 1914 and 1918. The ambulance was presented in February 1921.

The Armistice signed on the morning of 11 November 1918 ended the war in which three-quarters of a million soldiers had died. As the guns boomed out at 11 o'clock in the morning people abandoned their work in offices and shops, crowds poured out into the streets to sing and dance; whistles blew, and bells rang.

The peace treaty was signed on 28 June 1919, and peace was celebrated on 19 July 1919. Processions with decorated drays passed through the centre of the town. There was a terrible epidemic of septic influenza which swept through Europe and on around the world. In the United Kingdom there were 200,000 deaths.

At the church-yard gate, a lantern cross in memory of those who had lost their lives. The head is decorated with sculptures of the Crucifixion, the Madonna, St George and St Michael.

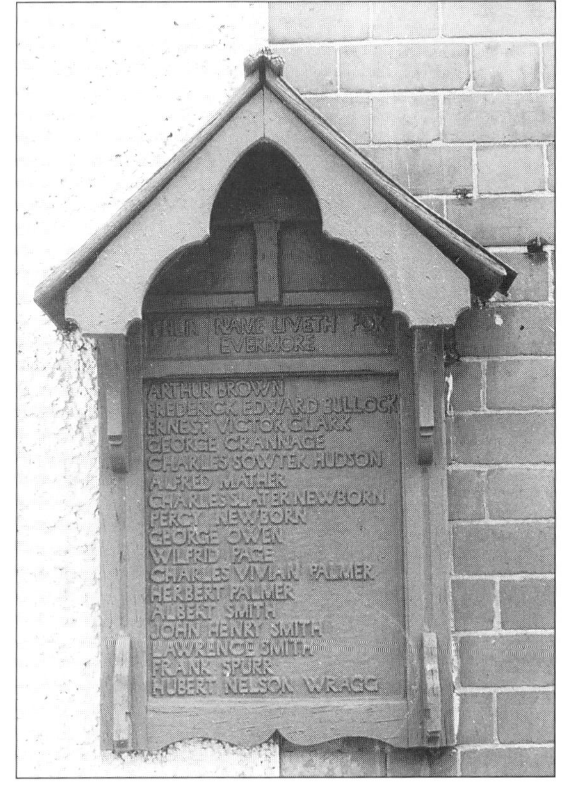

In Hamilton Road, a memorial commemorates the dead from that single street. A reminder of the terrible price paid by working people, and of the community spirit once so strong in the valley towns.

From the family albums of the 1920s, 'Banjo Jack' Wale. After the First World War he entertained with his banjo, especially for members of the British Legion. His grand-daughter likes to tell of the occasion when he was on stage with a donkey, which of course disgraced itself.

Three

Between the Wars

A first wireless set for Long Eaton, vintage 1923. The first public radio broadcast in Britain was made by Gugliecmo Marconi in February 1920. Arriving in England in 1898, he established his wireless company at Hall Street, Chelmsford. His success brought about the founding of the British Broadcasting Corporation and Lord Reith was appointed General Manager. Radio, or the 'wireless' as it was called, featured regular news bulletins, read in London and broadcast simultaneously from all regional stations. Listening to the radio was at first not a simple pleasure. It involved crystal sets, 'cat's whiskers', ear phones, aerials, and everyone else in the house keeping quiet.

Soon the valve-set surmounted by a loudspeaker enabled the whole family to listen and enjoy programmes together. Apart from listening to the regular news bulletins, there was Woman's Hour at 2 o'clock and Children's Hour at 5 o'clock, introduced by 'Uncles' and 'Aunties'. There were programmes on gardening, literary critics on books, and James Agate on the theatre. Christopher Stone talked about new classical records just appearing, and on 13 August 1927 Sir Henry Wood's promenade concerts were taken over by the BBC. A Christmas message was broadcast in 1932 by King George V for the first time, followed by a 'Round the Empire' programme which became a national institution.

Basil Halliday and his Broadcasting Band at the Rialto/Mayfair Ballroom. This band played six nights at the Oxford Street Ballroom, and broadcast every six weeks on the long-gone BBC Midland Home Service at its Broad Street, Birmingham studios. The band also appeared at various towns throughout the Midlands for other dances and concerts. This photograph from 1953 shows Bill Roberts on bass; Ron Allen, Eric Wiltshire, and Dennis Searby on trumpets; vocalist Danny Proctor and pianist Ken Humphries; Jack Rudd on drums; Ralph Bancroft, John Marshall and Terry Caine on saxes; with Basil Halliday, the leader, on alto sax.

The familiar 'tin trunk' as it was known, due to its sombre trunk-like appearance. The Palace Theatre, situated in Queen Street, became the venue for barn-storming companies and almost every type of theatrical entertainment was presented there prior to the 'bioscope', as the early cinematograph was known.

'Vint's Picturedrome', built in 1907 and known as the St James Theatre. It was leased to Mr Leon Vint in 1910, who introduced pictures and variety turns. In 1918, Gracie Fields and Archie Pitt appeared in two musical revues here. An extract from a letter received shortly before Miss Fields' death reads, 'I certainly remember working in Long Eaton, finishing a show there the first week which had been on the road for just over two years, so we were familiar with every joke and song. The second week, we had all new jokes and songs to get used to playing. I remember the try-out was dreadful, but the Long Eaton audiences must have been extra kind and gave us all encouragement, because that second show played for four years across the British Isles, Mr Tower of London was its name'. In 1923, Gracie Fields in the Alhambra Revue, London: Mr Tower of London.

Opposite: *Boys' Cinema* was published weekly, presenting famous film heroes with a photograph and biographical notes on the back. These four are from a set dated 1922. By 1937, Gaumont British owned 345 cinemas, Associated British Cinemas owned 431, Odeon 900, and 3,000 were privately owned.

WALLACE REID.

CHARLES HUTCHINSON.

TOM MIX. *(Fox.)*

CHARLIE CHAPLIN.

Rudyard Kipling's father, when a young man, was employed as an artist in the China Works at Burslem. In the happy days of his courtship many visits were made to Rudyard Lake, a popular venue for charabanc outings. It was in consequence of the parents' pleasant memories of these outings that the son received his Christian name.

Employees of Vida Artificial Silk Elastics, numbering 350, arriving at Blackpool for their annual works outing on Saturday 14 September 1929, the train having left Long Eaton station at 6.20am. The railways increased mobility and the introduction of the excursion train, a form of travel associated with Mr Thomas Cook of Melbourne, enabled people to travel cheaply in parties. Factory outings, Sunday School treats and similar occasions enabled special fare reductions to be made. The seaside resort found itself invaded by the masses, as did stately homes like Chatsworth House, or a Spa town like Matlock Bath. The Factory Act of 1833 stated that those under eighteen years of age should be entitled to eight half-days each year, as well as Christmas Day and Good Friday. The Bank Holiday Act of 1871 and subsequent legislation gave six Bank Holidays and many workers were given Saturday afternoons off.

A replica of Barton Transport's early bus, used for ferrying visitors to the famous Nottingham Goose Fair.

The royal princess, Elizabeth Alexandra Mary, born to the Duchess of York at 17 Bruton Street, London, on Wednesday 21 April 1926. Now began the reign of 'Princess Lilibet'. There were Lilibet hats and rompers, and dolls. Her every action was reported, collectors made up scrap-books of newspaper cuttings and picture postcard photographs. Twenty-six years later she was to be proclaimed Queen Elizabeth the Second.

'After the war the world finds itself impoverished, England is no longer the workshop of the world. European countries are too poor to import from us, lack of foreign trade, machine production, and the emancipation of women swell the unemployment figure, prices rise and whole areas are stricken with depression. The practical application of inventions such as the aeroplane, motor car, wireless and cinematograph, change man's habits and his material surroundings. Electric power and improved transport give a new mobility to industry, resulting in an enormous growth of existing centres of population, especially in the Midlands'. In December 1932 a Civic Appeal was made to all people of goodwill, the launching of the Long Eaton Unemployment Welfare Fund. A scheme had been inaugurated in cooperation with the Town Council, the religious bodies of the town, the Rotary Club, the Chamber of Trade, Toc H, the Trades Union Organisations, and others to help the unemployed of the town. 'In the general industrial depression now prevailing, it is keenly felt that every effort should be made to improve the conditions of unemployment in our midst, and to assist in providing a Welfare Centre for them. With the help and permission of the Town Council we are opening within a very short time, the buildings at the Tamworth Road Depot as a Welfare Centre and Workshop'.

A visitor to the workshop in 1935 was HRH the Duke of Kent, who in the previous year had married Princess Marina of Greece, their marriage in Westminster Abbey was the first royal wedding to be broadcast. The princess brought with her two items of interest to the fashion scene when she arrived in England. The 'Marina hat', a pill box hat that she wore, which immediately became all the rage. Within two weeks of her arrival copies were on sale for 2s 11d, and the colour Marina blue, a subtle shade of turquoise, is still popular sixty years later.

Long Eaton Rotary Club. Founder members in the first year of the Club, 7 June 1928, during a visit to Fort Dunlop.

The National Greyhound Racing Society was formed in 1927, and the first racing track was at Belle Vue, Manchester. The track at Long Eaton was opened shortly after. In 1948 the greyhound stadium was practically destroyed by a blaze, thought to have been started by sparks from a passing steam train. Fortunately, forty dogs were rescued from the blazing kennels, an act which brought five firemen PDSA certificates. Pictured with one of his winners is Mr Reg Barker of High Street, Long Eaton.

Redcourt, Derby Road, Long Eaton. The view from the main gates. 'Redcourt: for sale by auction. J.P. Newton and Sons. Zion Hall, Tuesday 9 May 1933. 7pm prompt'. (*Long Eaton Advertiser*, 5 May 1933).

The interior in the 1920s.

The interior seventy years later.

The wood carvings inside were the work of Mr Thos Alliott, photographed with his wife and family. Mrs Alliott, the former Miss MarGerrison, was well known at the Co-operative Restaurant. A picture from the old family album shows her wearing her hat, decorated with a feather, a gift from Mrs Claye of Bellfield House. Their son Donald, an accountant, was well known at British Celanese, their daughter became Mrs Walter Gregory of Chilwell Mark Roses and young Kenneth became a master plumber in the town.

The old butcher's shop on the corner of Regent Street.

Hilton's booteries on High Street.

The almshouses on High Street on the corner of Cross Street.

Boots the Chemists, which replaced them.

Looking along the High Street with Warners sweet shop on the left-hand side and Buttons Ironmongery on the corner of Howitt Street, now Greenwoods the men's outfitters. The Maypole Dairy has gone and in the middle of the block is W.H. Woolworths store. Wittering's shoe shop is on the corner of Gibb Street. The Empire Cinema had not yet been built on the corner of Orchard Street.

A close-up of Trent House, which later became Melias, Currys, and Roses Shoes.

The town's biggest menace — water. Flood water rose so rapidly in February 1946, that many families were too late to move furniture upstairs. A food distribution centre was set up at the Empire Cinema.

On the High Street, the Maypole Dairy, Woolworths 3d and 6d stores and the Witterings shoe shop with water too close for comfort.

On Derby Road, Stanhope Street is awash; during other floods the water has been very much deeper. There was cooperation from the Army, Home Guard, Sea Scouts, Sea Cadets, and Red Cross in distributing food. The Royal Air Force loaned rubber dinghies. In Mikado Road and Charnwood Avenue, houses had four feet of water in them. In bungalows the residents took refuge in the rafters. Dr J.P. Denny visited the sick in an army lorry and was then carried pick-a-back into the houses.

Tamworth Road, with the old fire station, the grammar school, and St James church surrounded by water.

The Market Place, with the Corner Pin reflected in the water — pity the postman with his parcel cart, and the market stall holders.

Four

New Beginnings

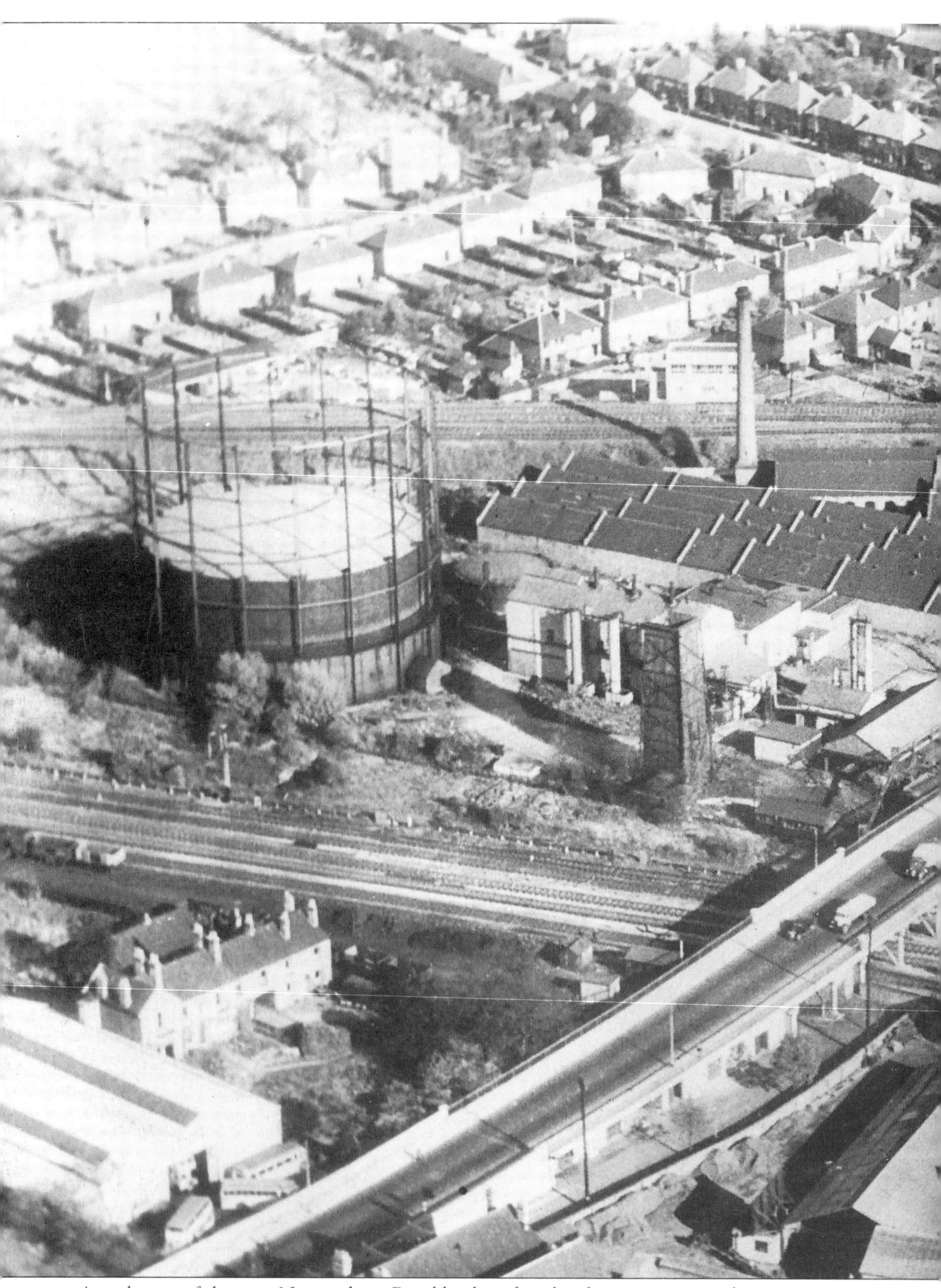

Aerial view of the new Nottingham Road bridge, shortly after it was opened.

Long Eaton's biggest problem solved, the hold up of traffic at railway crossings, especially the one on Nottingham Road, vehicles having to wait in queues for the passing of trains. The opening of the new Nottingham Road bridge solved the problem.

Music while you work. Workers on top of the gasometer enjoy listening to music from the concertina during their lunch-time break.

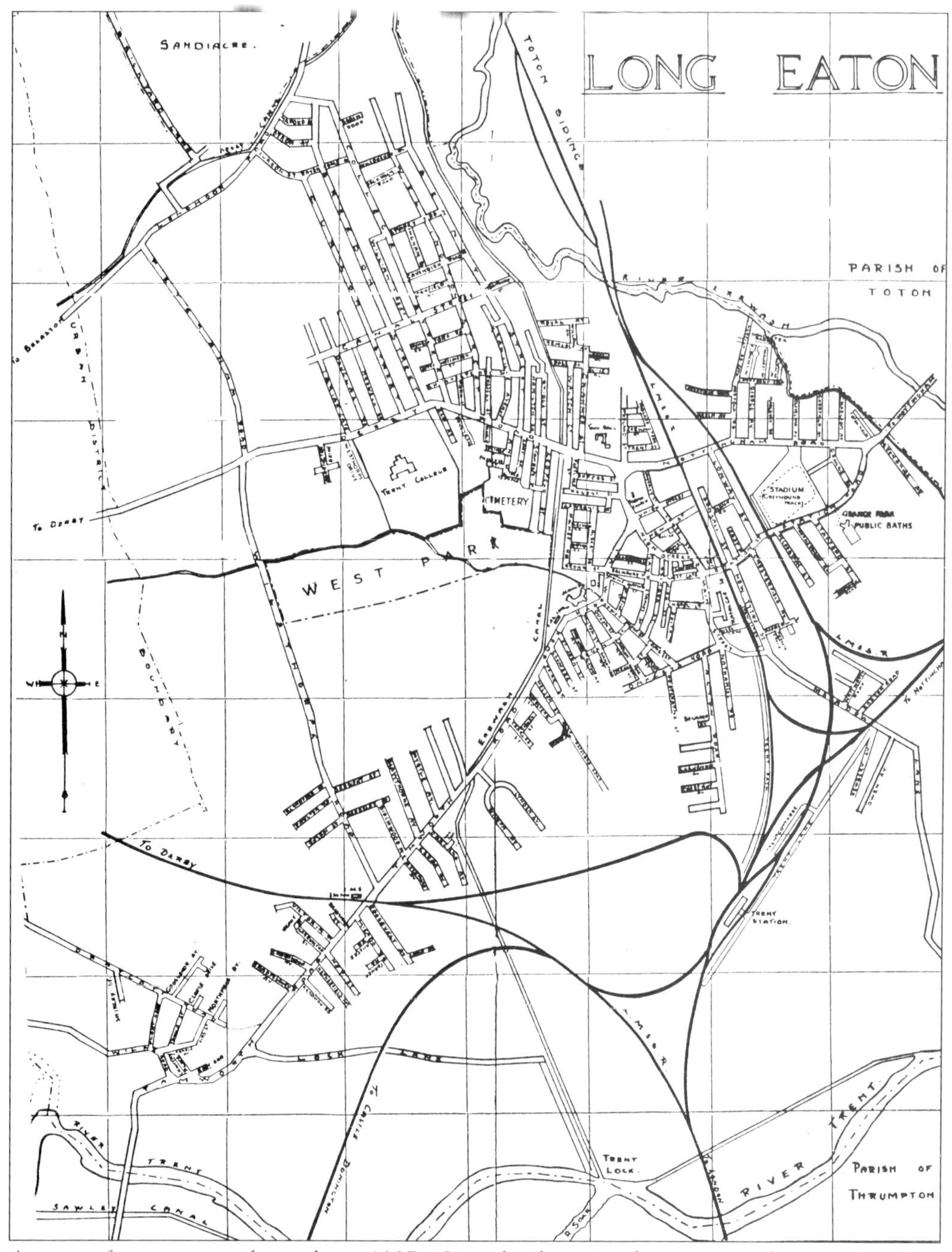

A copy of astreet map from about 1937. 'Sites for factories, low rents and rates, abundant labour. Main rail, road and water transport'. (Long Eaton Town Development Committee)

The grand opening of the NFD and DSS, Sawley Club Ltd, 31 May 1930.

The new public baths, opened by J.W. Comery Esq. (past Chairman of the Long Eaton Urban District Council) on Saturday 20 July 1935.

'For over a hundred years there has been a great desire for adequate facilities for swimming and bathing in the town. At no time has the subject appeared to be other than urgent. But the growth of a town is gradual; amenities come one by one, bringing with them responsibilities which have to be assessed before-hand and which a township must be prepared to carry once a scheme is launched'.

'The town's latest acquisition comprises a commodious, well-appointed and up-to-date building, replete with most modern accessories, and planted in a pleasant environment which is rapidly developing along happy, communal lines. Diving and spring boards are fixed at the deep end. The building at the North end contains Entrance Hall, Waiting Rooms, and six Slipper Baths for each sex. A pleasing feature at the South end is a Cafe with shelters on each side. A balcony above and an ornamental stone cascade in the foreground add both to the artistic effect and general utility'.

(Regd.)

'CARTELLEX'

INTERLOCK UNDERWEAR

LADIES, GENTS & CHILDREN

AND SPORTS WEAR

INTERLOCK
RAYON
SILK
UNDERWEAR
AND SPORTSWEAR

Ask for Our

LADIES', GENT'S & CHILDREN'S

BATHING COSTUMES

IN PURE WOOL

Fast Dye to Sea and Air

W. H. CARTER

OAKLEA MILLS, LONG EATON

The New "Cambridge" A Modern of the Moderns

NOW is the time to fit a New Grate before the Winter Comes . . . . . .

Modern Cookers from **£4 15s.**

Modern Tile Sets with oak mantels from **£4 4s.**

Over 100 sets to choose from

Ask for list of umbrellas, tables & tents, as supplied to the new baths.

J. & H. LACEY,

Ironmongers, Market Place & High Street

Tempting advertisements in the souvenir brochure: the modern fireplace compared to the old blackleaded grate (Erewash Museum).

Laceys staff pictured on their 25th anniversary in 1947. Back row: Syd Warren, George Curwood, Herbert Grebby, Syd Camp, -?-. Middle row: Andrew Young, George Varney, Bill Moore, Tom Rhodes, Mr Harvey, Philip Allen. Front row: Vera Deane, Sue Harvey, Jack Lacey, Harry Lacey, Jean Allen, Kate Ball. In front: Jeff Lewsley and Harry Walker.

Five

Leisurely Pursuits

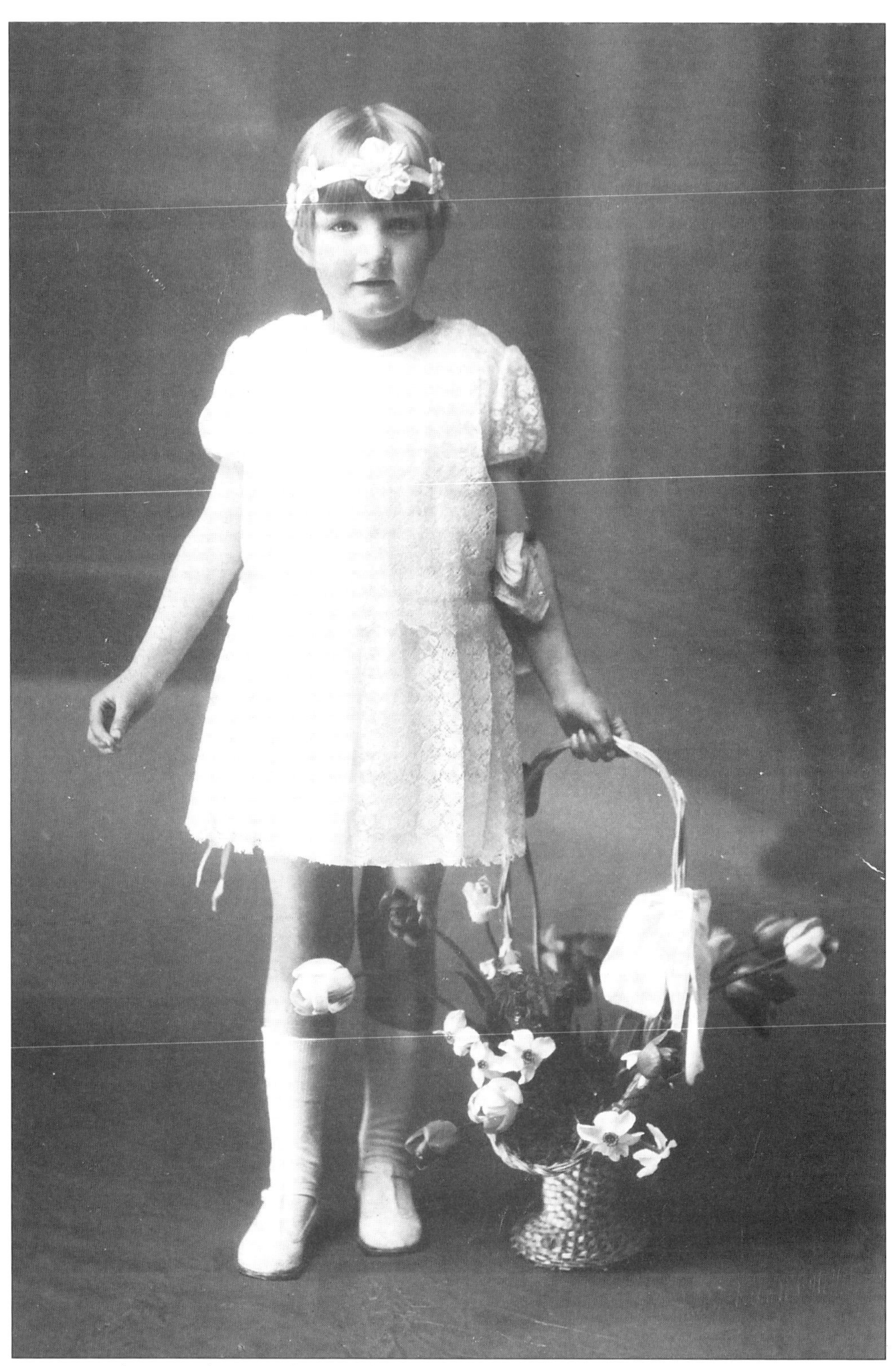

May Festival 1926. Olive Booth, attendant to the May Queen, now Mrs Jack Smith.

May Festival 1928. Irene Booth, attendant to the May Queen, Mrs H. Collinson.

During three days in May 1939, members of the Long Eaton Band of Hope Union staged their May Festival, featuring the operetta *Snow White and the Seven Dwarfs* under the musical direction of Mr Arthur Roberts. May Queen Miss Gwendoline Smith was the star attraction during the festival, while the lead role in the operetta was taken by Joyce Draycott.

At Carnival Time. 'Money must be raised for the local hospitals. The towns folk of Long Eaton showed their true metal. With carnival committees of over one hundred members, success had to be assured. Methods of raising additional money, apart from the street collections during the carnival processions, needed original ideas, which proved to be most successful'. (From Temperance Queen to Long Eaton Hospital's Carnival Queen, 1931).

Above: Olde worlde market stalls, and a Carnival Queen graced every function with great dignity, and thoroughly enjoyed every minute of it.

Local businessmen held to ransom — in the stocks. Hundreds of spectators gathered in the old Market Place to see eminent businessmen imprisoned in the stocks.

17

The Carnival of 1933. The celebrations ran for a week, from 9 to 16 September. 'There was always something going on, the whole town joined in and the atmosphere was wonderful'. There was a grand procession to launch the carnival, taking one-and-a-half hours to march from Trent Bridge in Old Sawley, along Tamworth Road to the Old Market Place in Long Eaton. Seventeen-year-old Iris Watts was the third Hospital Carnival Queen, and she was chosen as one of the eleven finalists by the Queen's Committee. She then had to audition before the Committee, reciting poetry. Her 'royal' duties involved attending all the different functions taking place throughout the week. She visited elderly people unable to leave their homes, and patients from Long Eaton in the hospitals in Nottingham and Derby.

Her crowning was performed by Miss Elizabeth Allen, the famous screen star; she was attended by her ladies in waiting, Joan Starkie (top left) and Doris Shingler (top right). Train bearers were Jean Smith (middle left) and Rita Walker (middle right), Bessie Cowlishaw (bottom left) and Betty Taylor (bottom right). The Queen and retinue visited Wellington Street School, her school. She was presented with a book of poems. Iris said, 'The headmistress, Miss Button, was really proud of me. She wanted all her girls to grow up as young ladies'. Each year, around £3-4,000 was made for Derbyshire Royal Infirmary and Nottingham's General Hospital, a staggering amount in the thirties.

Breaston Carnival, fun and frivolity in the cause of charity. Hospital Day is one in which folk give themselves unconstrainedly to the spirit of frivolity, underlying which is the deeper motive of aiding a worthy cause.

Crowning ceremony. The Sawley Carnival Queen, Miss Grace Astell, receiving her crown from Miss J. Horobin. Also present are the Carnival Queens of Shardlow and Breaston.

The crowning of the first Carnival Queen of Breaston, September 1937, was performed by Mrs G.A. Longden, of Draycott. Miss Ruth Lawley, the selected Queen, entered the arena with her attendants, Miss Mona Hird and Miss Mary Mills. The Carnival Queen, in delivering her declaration, called for loyalty and generous support for the twelfth Hospital Carnival the following Saturday. A display by the Ump-taggers Carnival Band, led by their mascot, Tagger the goat, followed. A junior and senior carnival band contest was arranged by Mr A.W. Perks. The winners were, Junior: 1st Back Bone of England. Seniors: 1st Nottingham Raleigh Ambassadors. Prizes for the best drum majors went to Ivan Alan of the Backbone of England and to the Raleigh Ambassadors Band. The 'Queen' made visits to the local hospitals, also to The Grove at Shardlow. Also taking part at Matlock Carnival were Carnival Queens from Heage, Bonsall, Darley Dale, Ripley and Youlgreave with their Maids of Honour.

The Backbone of England Band. Back Row: Dick Webb, Gordon Pelgrave, Teddy Archer, G. Hillier, Ken Cox, Ivan Allen, Glen Moody, Bert Freeman, -?-, Baz Butler, Teddy Burton. Centre row: Joyce Stenson, ? Watkins, ? Horobin, ? Adcock, ? Banstead, ? Smith, ? Butler, -?-, Adrey Twells, Vera Noon, Joan Jacklin, Joyce Watson, Mary Richards. Front Row: ? Hook, Geoff Butler, Bill Banks, Ivan Jacklin, John Noon, Beryl Freeman, Jessie Richards, -?-, ? Lowe, -?-, ? Hooks. In front, the Breaston Carnival Cup for the Smartest Drum Major, Ivan Allen.

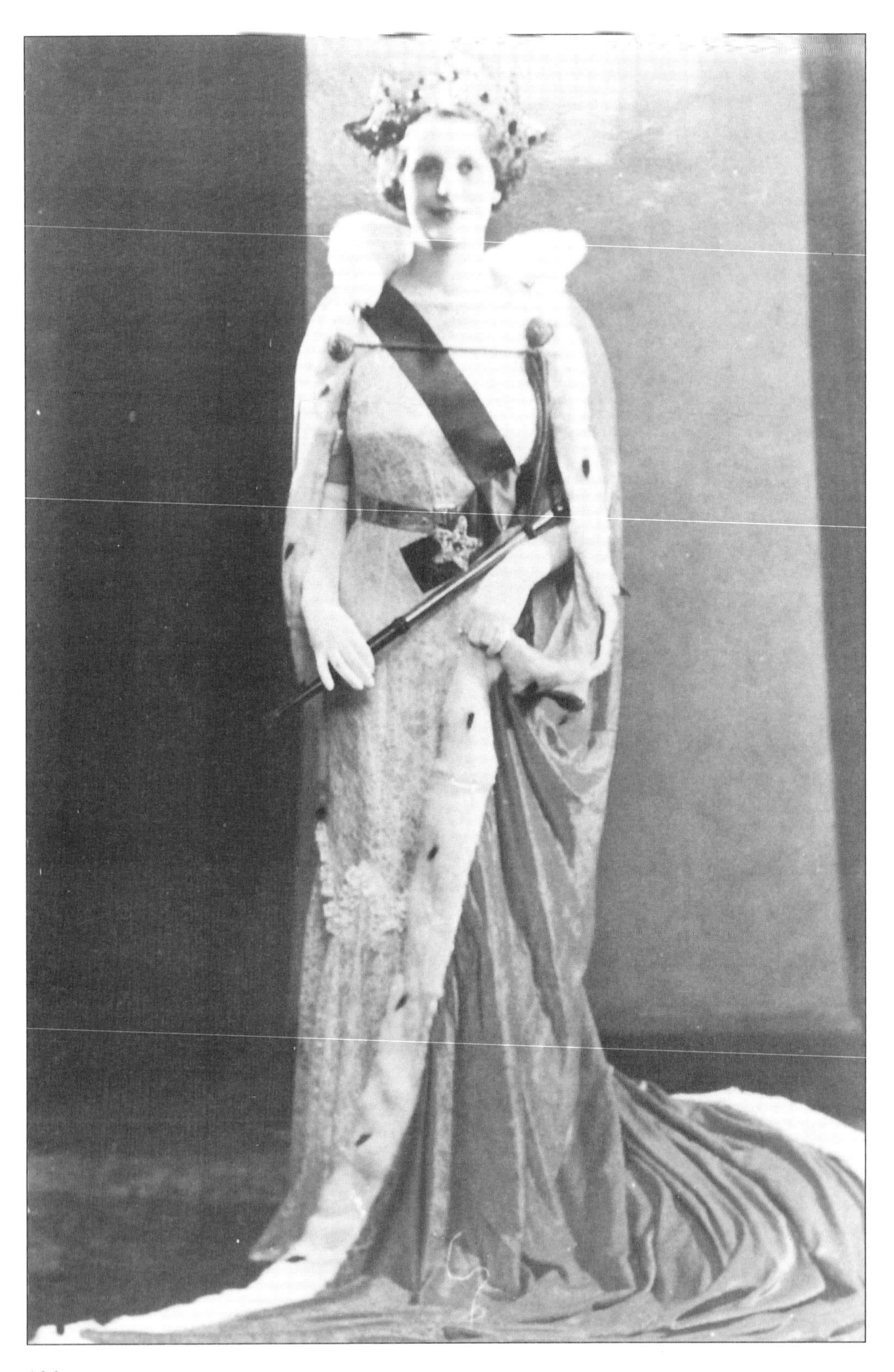

Taking part in the Thursday afternoon procession, half-day closing in the town, the Co-op float, with (left to right) Chris Robinson, Joan Tilson, Grace Hatfield, Iris Plackett, Mary Groves, Charlotte Beardsley, Joyce Yardley, Gertie Bagshaw, and driver, Ron Malvern.

Opposite: During a search-light tattoo on the tournament field at the top of Wilsthorpe Road, Miss Freda Hallam, the Carnival Queen of 1937, arrived in her interior-lit limousine, and was escorted around the arena. The crowning ceremony was a little different in the coronation years of King George VI and Queen Elizabeth: at the moment of crowning, all the attendants put on their coronets.

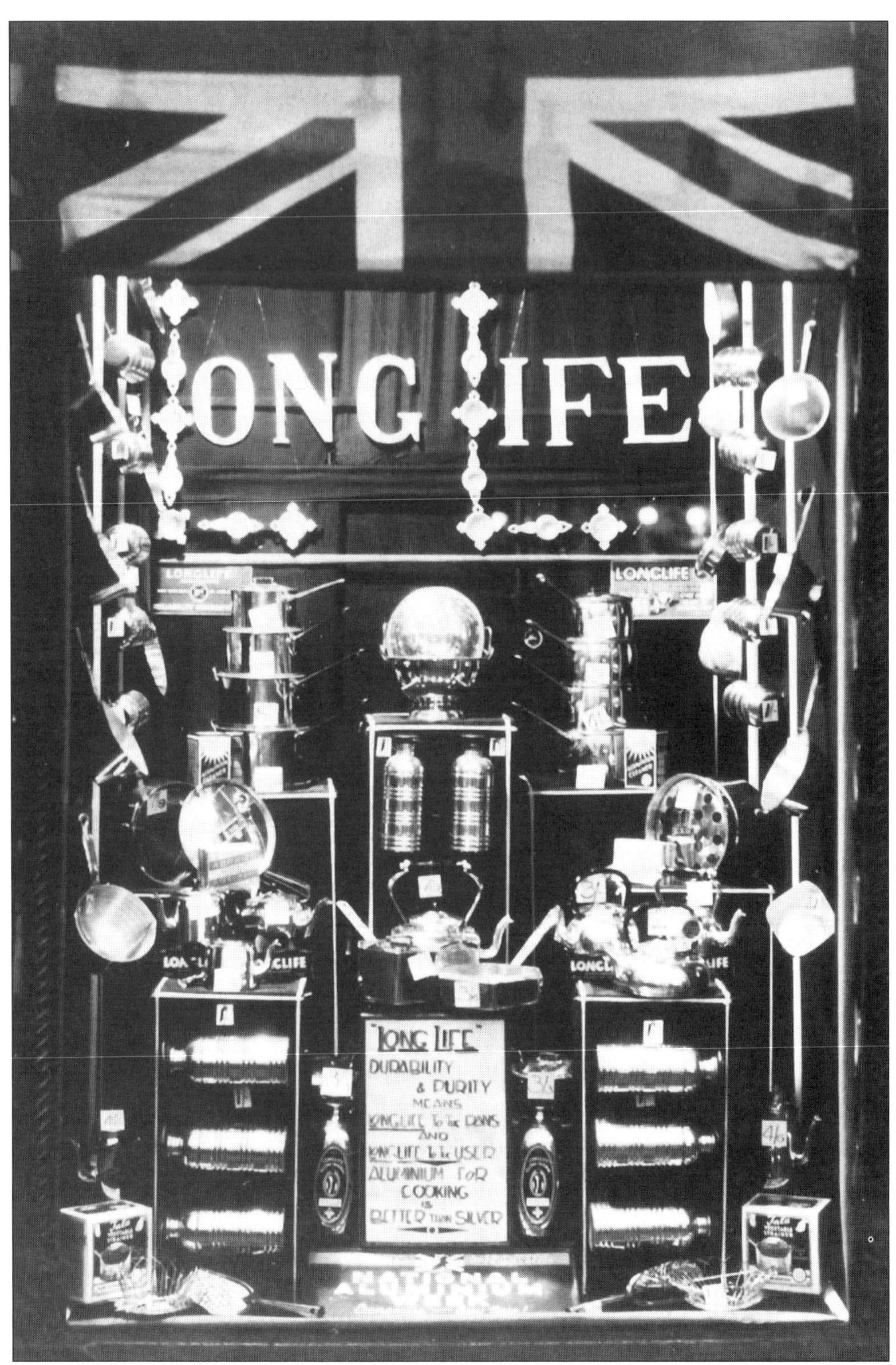

Laceys, noted for their eye-catching window displays, especially at carnival time.

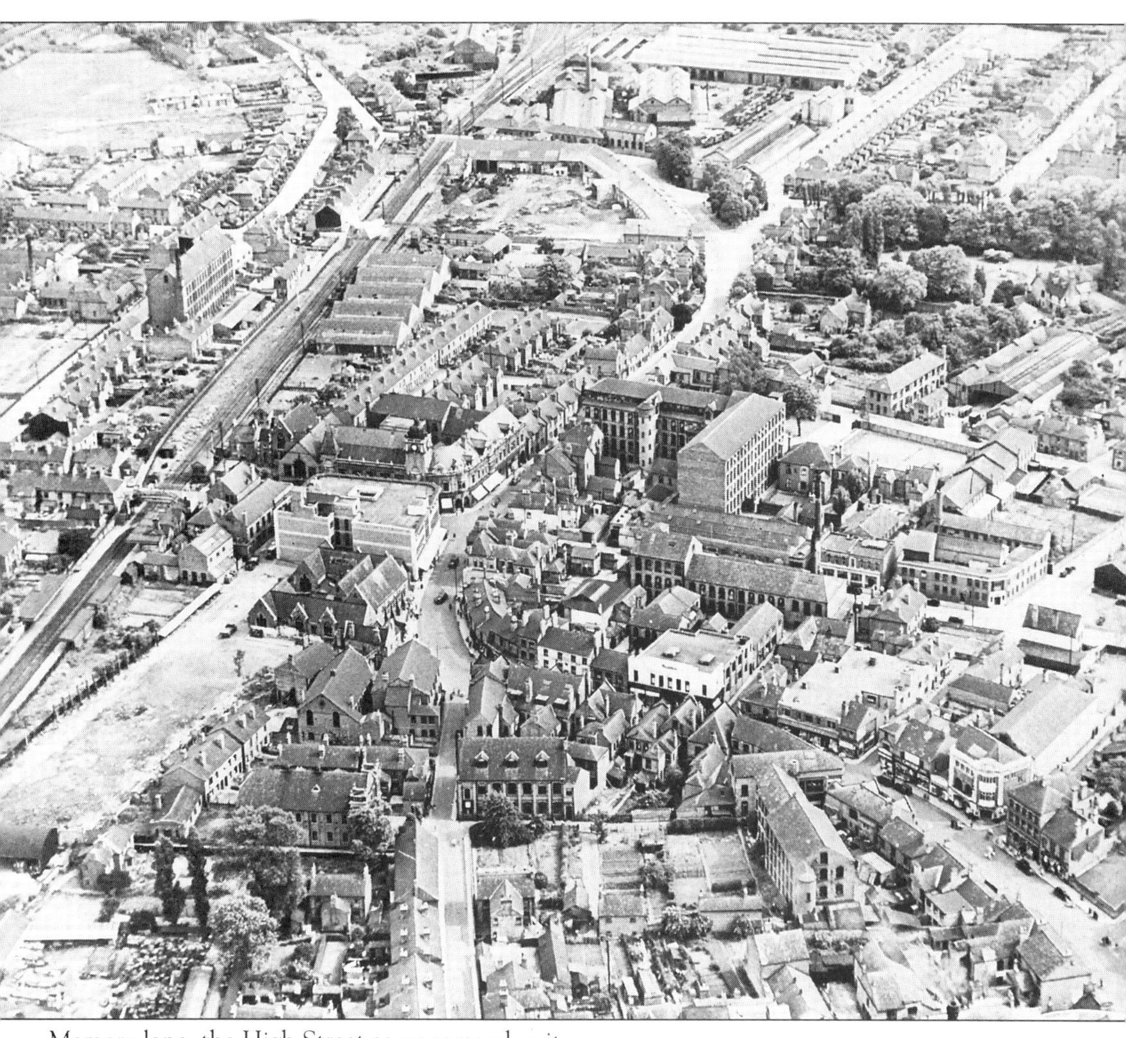

Memory lane: the High Street as we remember it.

A few steps down memory lane: the High Street. With the school and schooldays behind you, and your first wages in your pocket, a present for your parents, Boots the Chemists provided plenty of choice gifts, but with the princely sum of a little under ten shillings in 1938, one learned very early to be discriminating. Across the road the surgery, for Dr Denny and Dr Highfield, both, at one time or another, proclaiming you to be A1 after a medical examination.

A new store, Montague Burtons; Tom Mason, a master tailor but now the proud manager, a strict disciplinarian. Starched collars, black jacket and striped trousers, customers expected you to look immaculate — but the hours polishing that parquet floor, every day! Boarding suit lengths were on the display shelves. Here one also learned the art of window display and attention to detail, both in display and courtesy to the customer. Heads turned on the High Street when staff like Dick Gosling or Jack Wright were abroad. The pretty secretary, Peggy Philips, allowed me to persuade a youthful would-be Cecil Beaton to photograph her above the chimney tops, with the Co-op Clock Tower in the background.

Cigarette shortages. Irene Duckworth and Peggy's friend Mavis Atkin were in the Finlays tobacco kiosk. Can anyone ever forget asking for a packet of cigarettes when the quota for the day had been sold? On offer were some hideous, foul smelling objects in a packet, claiming to be aromatic 'Spanish Shawl'; to smoke them, we must have been desperate.

Cross Street, off High Street. The ghosts linger on where New Street crossed over. The old Police Station is no more. This shows the corner shop where Nurse Jowett, a well-loved Long Eaton character, was to be found. On the opposite corner was the hairdressing salon of Mr Heath (below), demolished like the police station. Outside the establishment are father and son and a very youthful Mr Blanchard, now with his own establishment at New Sawley.

Six

A World at War

Auxiliary Fire Service — sub station concordia. Below: (left to right) L.F. Cecil Frearson, F. Harry Jacklin, F. Fred Daft, F. Reg Fulwood, driver Sam Jackson, ARP Warden Bert Hirons, F. Sid Love, F. Frank Matchett, F. Frank Whitehead.

Members of NFS Station 3, Breedon Street.

Long Eaton First Aid Posts, formed in 1940 for the purpose of raising funds for local lads overseas. The Tournquets concert party raised approximately £2,500 towards parcels. The first performance was held at the Derby Road school baths. All the preparation was done after the children went home, taking two and a half hours to build the stage, erect the scenery and arrange the seats. All had to be dismantled afterwards, ready for classes the following day. Members of the cast of the pantomime *Cinderella* were Billy Goldsmith, who took part with his brother and Dickie Balding and Arthur Johnson; Buttons was played by Tommy Mulroy, and Dr Ritchie was the Dame. Harry Barber was in charge of music,

FOR FREEDOM
WAR SAVINGS CAMPAIGN 1944
PRESENTED BY THE WAR OFFICE
TO THE LOCAL SAVINGS COMMITTEE
IN APPRECIATION OF THEIR SUCCESS IN
SALUTE THE SOLDIER WEEK

1944, 'the year of miracles' and the beginning of the end, saw D-Day, doodle bugs, and Arnhem.

The first and last regiment, 4/7th Dragoons Title. An extract from the *Daily Telegraph* dated 5 June 1945 reads, 'By their deeds in battles over the last quarter of a century the 4/7th Royal Dragoon Guards will be known to the future Tank men as the first and last regiment. In 1918 their horses were the first across the Hohenzollern bridge over the Rhine into Germany. In September 1939 they were the first cavalry-turned-tank regiment to arrive with the B.E.F. On D-Day their specially waterproofed tanks were first ashore in Normandy. On Friday 4 May 1945 they were fighting side by side with the famous 51st Highland Division, the last British Troops in action against the Germans'. This is the Regimental Headquarters Squadron, the Colonel and members of Regimental H.Q. Tank Troop, official after-V.E. Day Parade photograph.

Lighter moments: *Black-Beret Pie*, a revue at the Tobi Theatre, Ochtrup, December 1945. The members of the band were troopers C. Horton, J. Hudson, G. Rose, J. Jordan, and K. Clarke. The regiment was encouraged to create its own entertainment by the Brigadier. The wide boy himself, Arthur English, was also producing a similar show with one of the squadrons. Chilwell, a mobilisation branch, was established to concentrate solely on the equipping of units as the War Office ordered their preparation for overseas. The Ordnance Field Parks and Workshops Stores Sections of many formations, such as the 1st Airborne, 6th Airborne, 51th Highland, 7th Armoured, 11th Armoured and Guards Armoured Divisions were equipped prior to the landing in Normandy. When members of the tank troop visited the Tank Park at Chilwell, they would have visited the Forces Canteen, at the Station Street Baptist Chapel.

The free world celebrates: VE Day, 8 May 1945. A street party, Friar Street. Note the street shelters; the second may be in Abbot Street. The end of the most deadly and ruinous war in history was marked by VJ Day, 15 August 1945, and in November the Nuremberg war crime trials opened. The War Office artist commissioned to cover the proceedings was Laura Knight. Laura Johnson was born in Long Eaton in 1877, marrying Harold Knight in 1903. Laura Knight, one of the leading women artists of the twentieth century, was a household name during her lifetime, and the first woman artist to be made a Dame of the British Empire. She is perhaps most famous for her captivating portrayals of London's theatre and ballet, and of the circus. Fairs and performances engaged her interest in the *exotica* of costume and scenery, but she was also attracted to the quiet moments backstage, behind the clamour of public enjoyment.

The amounts of food allowed in wartime rationing: sugar, 8oz. Butter, ham, bacon, 4oz of each. Tea, 2oz. Margarine, 2oz. Cooking fat, 2oz. Preserves varied between 8oz and 1lb per four weeks. Cheese was usually 3oz (with special rations for farm workers). Milk and egg rationing depended on age and priority status. Meat was rationed on a value basis, initially £1.10 per week (11d for the under-sixes). Confectionery and chocolate rations were 12oz per four weeks. At Christmas 1944, a special extra ration of 8oz was given to all children under 18.

A Christmas party at home, *c.* 1946. Back row: Bert Johnson, Ivan Jacklin, Mr Adcock, Bob Hodge, Bill Adcock, Gordon Mason, Jack Kilbourne. Middle row: Doreen Adcock, -!-, Audrey Mason, Marion Martin, Bill Wain, Winnie Wain, Mrs Adcock, Joyce Kilbourne, Mrs Martin. Front row: Bertha Berrisford, Mrs Johnson, Elsie Kilbourne, Mary Kilbourne, Edgar Kilbourne, Gwen Adcock, Kath Woolley.

Seven

Picking up the Pieces

A nativity play, Mount Tabor Sunday School, 1950. To those who have never seen the inside of the building, it at least gives an impression of the magnificent work of the craftsmen who helped to build it in 1884.

Methodist Youth Club, 7th birthday party, September 1949. Front row, seated: Mrs Lambley, Barbara Booth, Shirley Dewell, Brenda Wakeling, Doreen Sandford, -?-, Jocey Hunt, Audrey Whatton, Valerie Hickton, Audrey Wakeling, Sheila Wakeling, Derek Bagshaw. Second row, seated: Joan ?, her brother, Albert Henderson, -?-, Keith Turton, Beryl Beaumont, Alan Beaumont, Margaret Harding, Mrs Tingle, Revd Tingle, Revd Santry, Barbara Radford, Iris Toleman, -?-. Third row, standing: Mrs Fletcher, Bert Whatton, -?-, Mrs Brierly, Clare McFarlane, Mabel Whatton, Joyce Jowett, Margaret Patchet, June Torton, Sheila Offiler, Yvonne McFarlane, Anne Smith, Alan Woodcock, Keith Walton, A. Patchet, Zena Offiler, Maurice Barker, Eileen ?, Howard Fletcher, Peter Harris, -?-, Jean Wakeling, Cissie Goodwin, -?-, -?-, -?-, June Brierly, Barry Hickling, Mary Spyby, Charles Spyby. Back row, standing: Mrs Martin, 'Bobbie' Dewell, Bill Hoar, Keith Quiningborough, Jessie Hutchings, Les Fulwood, Gordon Earl, -?-, -?-, Mr Brierly, Mr Lambley, Joan Pape, Viv Pape, Eric Lambley, Jean Harding, Mrs Toleman, Mr Toleman.

Cadets of Temperance with their May Queen, Margaret Callandine, in 1949, with Drum Major Neville Sharp and chief attendant, Brenda Wakeling, who became May Queen in 1950.

Long Eaton Young People's Choir, 1976. Their conductor was Mrs Margaret Chambers, whose mother, Mrs Marie Cotton, used to be the pianist for the Band of Hope in Long Eaton. It was as an off-shoot of that organisation that the Young People's Choir was formed in April 1951. The first pianist was Mrs Cotton and the conductor was Mr Fred Wood. It had a fourteen-strong committee. Mr Wood was succeeded by Mr Arthur Roberts, and when ill-health forced him to resign Mr Roland Prentice took over. In those early days the choir concentrated mainly on competitive music festival events and scored many successes in the area. Mrs Chambers took over as temporary conductor in 1963 and under her leadership the emphasis changed from being competitors to entertainers, and in so doing they have brought much pleasure to hundreds of people.

High Street School's *The Gondoliers* produced in 1933 at The Peoples Hall. The cast: Mary Haddon, Mary Batchelor, Connie Taylor, Joan Sampson, Irene Baker, Grace Shipley, Grace Scott, Lilian Bradley, Dora Barker, ? Redgate, Hilda Hind, Doris Taylor, Edith Baker, Nellie Baker, Joan Arlott, Winifred Davis, Winnie Shepherd, ? Beardsley, Vera Black, Evelyn Gilder, Doris Robotham, Joan Gamble, Penny Limington.

High Street School, *Iolanthe*, 1937. Where it all started — with a children's production. The leading members of the cast were: Lord Chancellor, Gordon Booth; Earl Montararat, Stanley Roberts; Earl Tolloller, Jack Keighley, Private Willis, Ernest Miles; Strephon, Benjamin Hartley; Iolanthe, Irene Norton; Phyllis, Joyce Draycott; Fairy Queen, Beryl Wall; Celia, Audrey Cross; Leila, Megan Barker; Fleta, Winnie Lemmons.

The chorus of peers. High Street School, *Iolanthe*, produced in April 1937 at The Peoples Hall. *Derby Evening Telegraph*'s 'Man in the Stalls' wrote at the time, 'For children all under 14 years of age to perform in its entirety a Gilbert and Sullivan opera seems at first well nigh impossible. I was more interested because the producer and musical director was Mr Harold Newbury, whose enthusiasm for and ability in Gilbert and Sullivan opera is well known. I was lost in admiration for the way in which Mr Newbury handled his large chorus of 80 children, and encouraged each of his principles to give of his best'.

The chorus of fairies.

Long Eaton High Street with Grange (Old Scholars). The Gilbert and Sullivan Amateur Operatic Society presents *The Mikado*. In 1885 Gilbert and Sullivan scored with *The Mikado*, opening at the newly-built Savoy Theatre under the direction of Richard D'Oyley Carte. The songs were favourites in every drawing room. Seventy years later at The Peoples Hall, Long Eaton, Ken Godfrey stars in the title role of the Mikado, with George Cheshire as Nanki-Poo; Ron Smith, Ko-Ko; Frank Wightman, Pooh-Bah; Dennis Gibbs, Pish-Tush; Joyce Heath, Yum-Yum; Peggy Decker, Pitti-Sing; Marney Thomas, Peep-Bo; Antoinette Craig, Katisha; Teresa Dunham, Ko-Ko's attendant. The orchestra: 1st violins: H. Birks, E. Kilbourne, I. Jacklin; 2nd violins: H. Clarke, H. Akers; cello: F. Cowlinshaw, J. Kilbourne; bass: W. Bartin; flute: V. Needham; oboe: A. Syson; clarinet: R. Bosisto; bassoon: L.E. Winfield; trumpet: E. Crowe; percussion: F. Groves; pianist: Mrs E.M. Kilbourne; conductor: Harold Newbury, Esq.

The Long Eaton Co-operative Society. A great scheme of re-building and modernisation was decided upon and the new 'Emporium' was officially opened on Saturday 21 September 1935.

Across Station Street, on a field with trees and shrubs, the second part of the New Central was opened in 1900. Electricity was installed, and above the shops The Peoples Hall was opened. The largest public meeting hall in the district, it was used for all manner of purposes ranging from dances to civic banquets, from members' meetings to the paying-out of dividends, from dramatic and musical performances to election rallies.

The Board of Directors and Officials. Back row: Mr Walter Wall, Cllr E.W. Roper, Mr S. Castledine, Mr P.P. Davis. Middle row: Mr E. Wall, Mr A.E. Preston, Mrs Styles, Mr W.P. Taylor, Mr W. McCracken, Cllr A. Yates. Front row: Mr M.W. Angrave, Cllr L. Pattison, JP, Mr J.A. Ward, Mr A.E. Wigginton, Mr W.E. Crisp.

Directors and officials, 1946. Back row: Mr A.E. Corby, Mr E. Hemsley, Cllr G.A. Sharpe, Mr W.F. Ward, Mr W.P. Taylor, Mr F.B. England, Mr A. Wyatt C.C., Mr W. McCracken. Front row: Mr D.D. Lawton, Mrs A.E. Roberts (Vice-President), Mr C.U. Thomas (General Manager), Cllr A.E. Wiggington, JP (Secretary), Mrs M.J. Worthington, Cllr E.W. Roper. Aubrey Wyatt was a director of the Board from 1942 to 1965, an unbroken record of service until he retired under the age rule.

In the Diamond Jubilee Year, 1928, the new Model Dairy in Meadow Lane was built to replace the old Oakleys Road dairy, where about 6,000 gallons of milk per week were received from thirty farmers and the Co-op's own three farms. 'New plant to be installed at the new dairy will be capable of dealing with 500 gallons of milk per hour under the most hygienic methods'.

Long Eaton Co-op Fire Brigade, 1929. Back row: H. Longdon, ? Horrobin, G. Gascoigne, T. Osborne, ? Symington, J. Beer. Front row: R. Davis, B. Lovett, Cllr J. Pattison, ? Wheeldon, S. Smith.

A memorial erected by the employees and directors at The Peoples Hall, to the memory of the sixteen employees who fell in the First World War, it was unveiled on 13 March 1924. The Revd C.L. Vinson conducted a most impressive service, which was attended by relatives and friends and employees. The memorial, the work of Mr Thos Alliott, one of the employees in the Co-op Boot Repairs Department, was unveiled by another employee, Mr M. Bowd.

The Long Eaton Co-operative Senior Prize Choir. In the dark days of the 1930s, as the clouds of war were gathering, musicians Louis and Connie Patterson decided to brighten the outlook by forming a choir for members of the Co-op, with regular concerts at The Peoples Hall. To add variety they would occasionally introduce short sketches or a one-act play into the programme. Thus, the 'Arcade Players' came into being. The name was taken from the rehearsal venue, a large room, later the Countryman restaurant, over the Co-op Arcade in the Market Place. When war eventually broke out and many of the men were called up, it was left to the women to keep the flag flying at home until they returned. It is thanks to these, the ladies of the Senior Choir, that the group exists today.

Prize-winners in local drama festivals, 1966. Back Row: May Stringfellow, Betty Walker, Susan Perry, Mary Clarke, Jeanette Speake, Irene Millington, Pat Constable, Margaret Player. Middle row: John Barker, Gilbert Harding, David Nall, Richard Poyser, George Cheshire, John Harding, Ernest Speake, Trevor Singleton, Ted Player, -?-. Front row: Gladys Brookes, Vi Clementson, Alice Wright, Audrey Nall, Yvonne Raven, Tom Perry, Gillian Culley, Hazel Hillier, Stan Weatherill. Seated on floor: -?-, Jeanne Lewis, Barry Culley, Mary Wildbore, June Groocock, John Constable, June Barker.

This Happy Breed, 1958. Standing: Ted Player, May Stringfellow, Jean Daft, John Brecknock, John Constable, Joe Ferrier, Audrey Nall, Pat Smith, Tom Perry. Seated: Alice Wright, June Jones, June Barker.

Book of the Month, 1957. Back row: June MarGerrison, John Brecknock, Maureen Shipstone, Ted Player. Front row: June Groocock, Joe Ferrier, Joan Robinson, Barry Cully.

The Colonel and the Maid. On stage there always had to be an embarrassing moment for someone. False moustaches have been known to transfer from one face to another during a passionate embrace. It had to happen during *Book of the Month*. Colonel Howard Barnes-Bradley, an amorous gentleman, is having an affair with the Maid, Doris. After a tender kiss, he surfaces bare-faced, his moustache having accidently become an extra adornment for Doris. The audience enjoyed it.

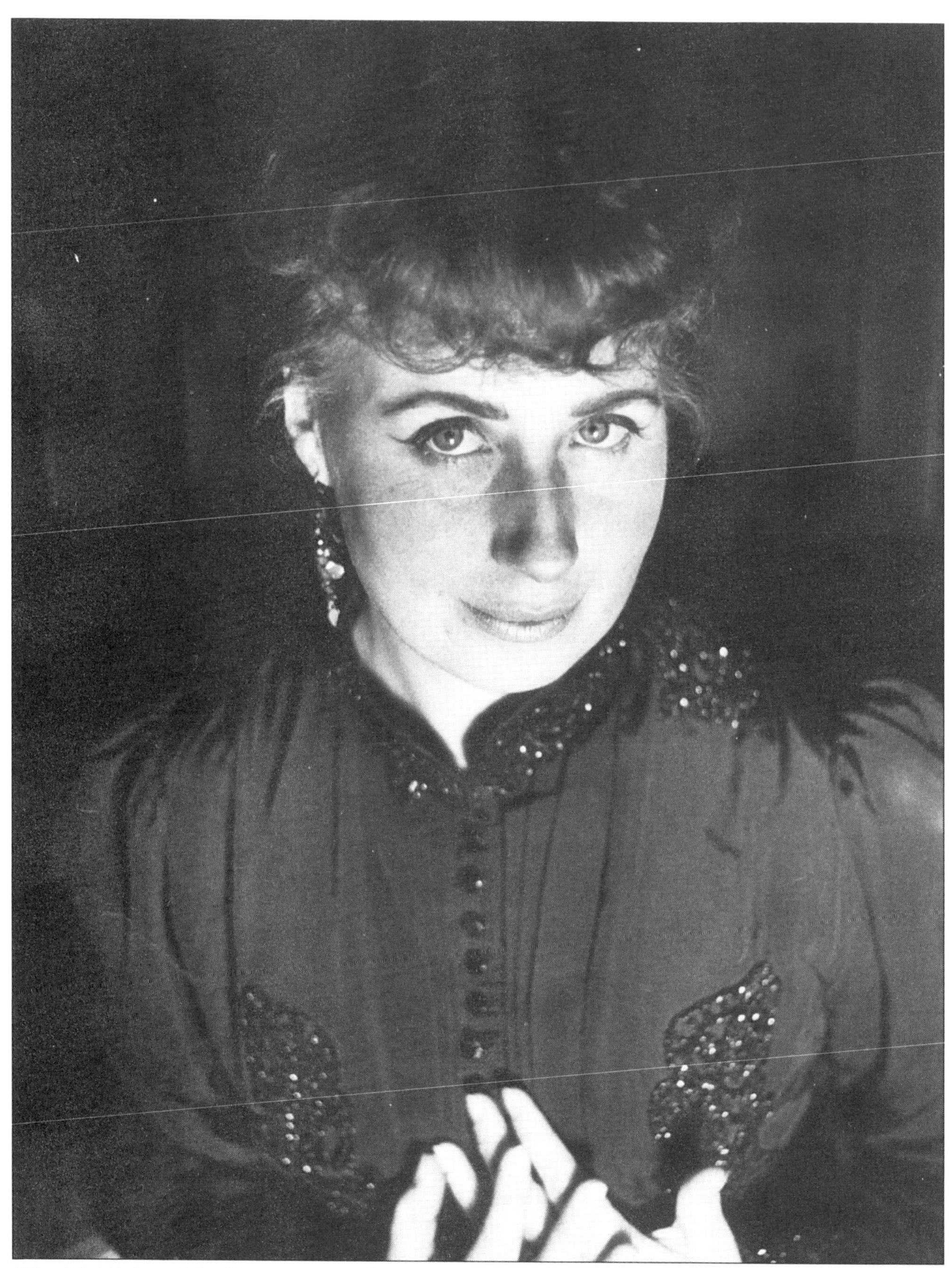

'The Maid', June MarGerrison, stays home, marries and enjoys taking parts in plays and playing in Old Time Music Hall, with the Same Lot As Last Time, helping to raise thousands of pounds for charity over the years with Peter Colton and Tony Gregory and company.

'The Colonel', John Brecknock, started in the Arcade Players and was bitten so badly by the performing 'bug' after playing crooner in the 1956 production of *As Long As They're Happy*, that he went professional, studying singing in the Birmingham School of Music and eventually achieving operatic stardom and appearing in the great opera houses of the world, as well as on the radio and television. He is now semi-retired and lives with his German wife, Lora, in their villa in Spain. He appeared in *La Cenerentola* at Teatro Colon, Buenos Aires.

Ruddigore, 1949. The Co-op Quire became EDACRA Music Society and they are now about to celebrate their centenery in 1995 as the Erewash Music Scoiety.

The Mikado, The Peoples Hall. Another opening, another show. Back row: -?-, George ?, Harry Mellors, -?-, Dennis Bagguley, Ernest Hall, George Ratclyft. Middle row: Penny Frost, Hilda Hollingsworth, Holly Croft, Margaret Mellors, ? Moore, John Croft, Frank Barker, Les Frost, -?-, Moreen Birks, Winnie Roberts, -?-, Eileen Wood, -?-, Ted Birch, Jim Hindle. Front row: Lily Chapman, Arthur Ratclyft, May Marriott, -?-, Kathleen Tomlinson, Jean Poules, Nellie Harrison, Rose Hill, -?-, Miriam ?. Kneeling: Cyril Scott, Nellie Scott. Members of the orchestra: Edgar Kilbourne, Harry Birks, Nellie Bosisto, Bernard Bandley, and Vic Needham.

Iolanthe, 1958. M. Rose, N. Robey, M. Large, K. Davies, J. Rockley, Moreen Birks, P. Symington.

The Yeomen of the Guard, 1961, Long Eaton Operatic Society. Sergeant Merryll, D. Gibbs; Dame Carruthers, Antoinette Craig; Colonel Fairfax, George Cheshire; Elsie, Barbara Cheshire; Phoebe, Morva Lawrence; Jack Point, Ken Godfrey; Wilfred, D. Maltby.

From the family album — a young violinist, Harry Birks, August 1911.

The Merry Widow, 1969 (EDACRA). B. Shaw, D. Allen, Jean Bishop, K. Godfrey, Henry Middleton.

Half a Sixpence, 1984 (Erewash Music Society), the principles and chorus.

In the Picture. Twenty years after Benjamin Britten had founded his Festival of Music and the Arts at Aldeburgh, Mr Philip Setterfield, the music master at the Grammar School, suggested that Long Eaton, with the abundance of talent available, might hold a similar annual event. In 1968 the Festival Revue Company was formed, happily with considerable success. Here Alice Wright and Dennis Bagguley join Pat and Bill Farmer, with Molly Wright and Gillian Bates in the revue sketch *In the Picture*.

Nurse Amelia Brentnall, of the well-known farmers and butchers in the Market Place. She is photographed here with some of the young performers who helped in her productions to raise money for the St Laurence Waifs and Strays.

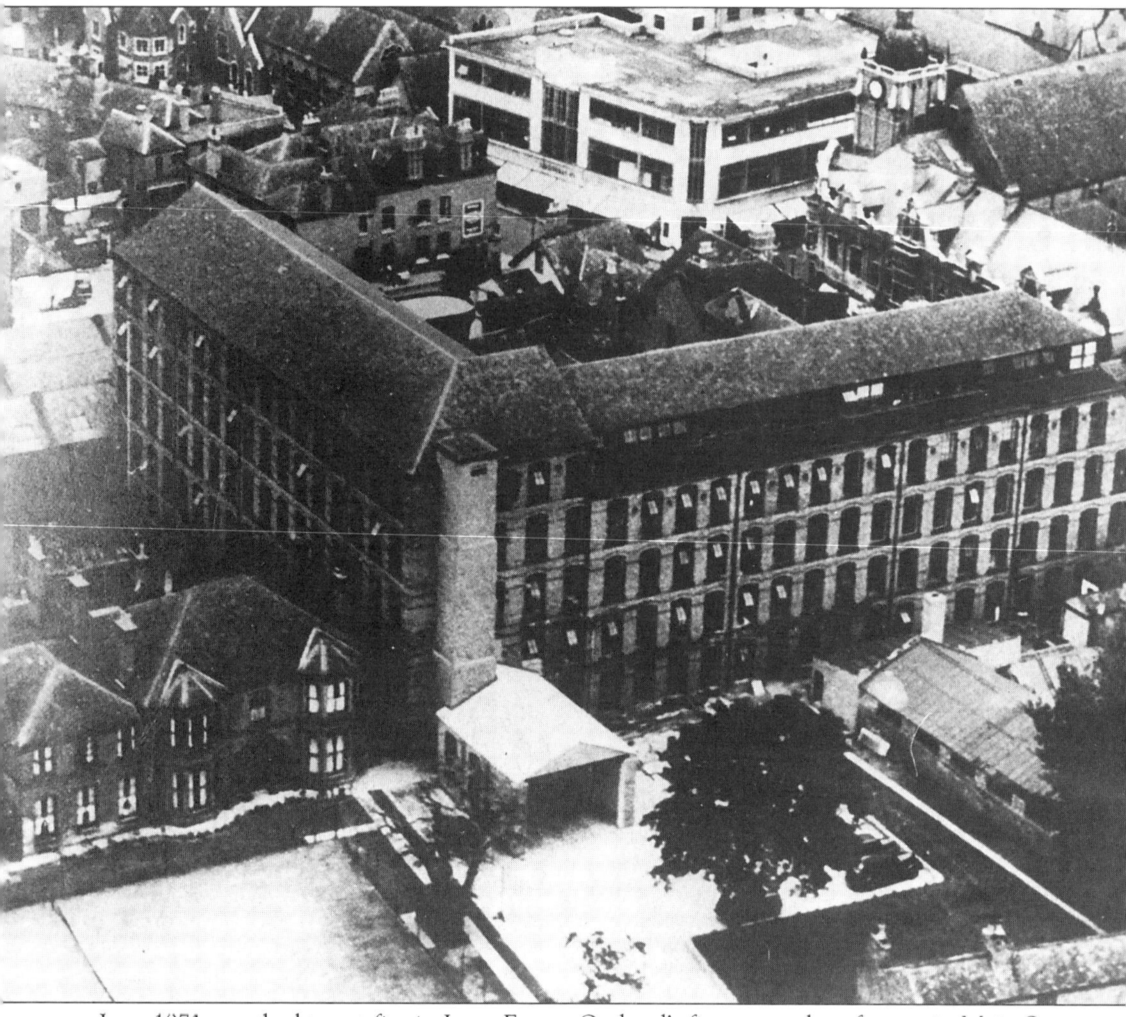

June 1971 saw the biggest fire in Long Eaton, Orchard's five-storey lace factory in Main Street caught fire. Over one hundred and fifty firemen from four brigades were called in with twenty-two pumps, four turntable ladders and two salvage tenders. Latterly known as the 'Tea Factory' it took firemen three weeks to damp down the remains.

The town crier's bell rings again, at Long Eaton carnival, 1979. Well-known local actor and singer Ken Godfrey takes to the streets of the town with the old bell, announcing the carnival events and declaring the proceedings open on West Park.

The carnival procession winds through the old Market Place. The market stalls have been moved to a new site; another move for them is envisaged as we approach a new century.

The Friendship Quilt, 1980. An idea suggested by needlecraft students of the Long Eaton, Breaston and Sandiacre Adult Education Centres has resulted in busy, nimble fingers making patchwork rings for a quilt. The name of this design in patchwork is called The Dresden Plate of Friendship Ring, or simply, The Friendship Ring. Mrs Pauline Barke, the patchwork and embroidery teacher, supervised the work. When completed, the quilt was donated to the Long Eaton and District Arts Council to raise funds for the promotion of the arts in Long Eaton and district.